Humble Table, Wise Fare

Roots of the Dharma Series

Humble Table, Wise Fare

Gifts for Life

Venerable Master Hsing Yun

Translated by
Tom Manzo and Shujan Cheng

Authors Choice Press
San Jose New York Lincoln Shanghai

Humble Table, Wise Fare
Gifts for Life

All Rights Reserved © 2000 by Hsing Yun

No part of this book may be reproduced or transmitted in any form or by any
means, graphic, electronic, or mechanical, including photocopying, recording,
taping, or by any information storage or retrieval system, without the
permission in writing from the publisher.

Authors Choice Press
an imprint of iUniverse.com, Inc.

For information address:
iUniverse.com, Inc.
620 North 48th Street, Suite 201
Lincoln, NE 68504-3467
www.iuniverse.com

ISBN: 0-595-14372-5

Printed in the United States of America

Preface

The Vegetable Root Sayings is a Chinese book that was written by Hung Tz-Cheng during the Ming Dynasty. Since that time, numerous editions have been printed, with some copies being distributed for free. Some editions have contained graceful illustrations; a few years ago, the famous Taiwanese cartoonist Tsai Chih-Chung produced one such edition, complete with cartoons. I have also heard the book is currently widely distributed in Mainland China as well. These illustrated editions have increased the circulation of the book. The illustrations not only make the book more enjoyable to read, but also help people understand the principle of personal conduct. The merits from promoting the book's distribution are really boundless.

When I was young, I often read *The Vegetable Root Sayings*, familiarizing myself with the content of the book. Later, when I was preaching the Dharma, I was able to quote from the book. Over time, I have found that *The Vegetable Root Sayings* is not only brief, to the point, tactful and charming, but also rich in philosophical and literary gracefulness; it is popular and yet august. The literary and artistic meaning is so profound and lasting that each saying can serve as a motto for dealing with people and conducting affairs in daily life.

For more than thirty years, everything I have said and done has been for the purpose of preaching the Dharma and educating people's minds. Recently, it occurred to me that some of what I have said has the same style as *The Vegetable Root Sayings*, and that a collection of these could be dedicated to the youth of today to serve as a reference for cultivating body and mind. Joyfully aware of this possibility, some of my Fo Guang Shan disciples began to collect my lectures, diary entries,

Humble Table, Wise Fare

Dharma talks and opening speeches—more than 2,000 items in all. For the publication of *Roots of the Dharma* I have selected one thousand of these.

I have four hopes for this publication:
1. The content of this book is a selection of words that I have spoken to all levels of people. At this time our society is promoting spiritual reform. I sincerely hope that, by reading this book, people will feel the benefit of increasing merits and purifying the body and mind and consequently make some contribution to society.
2. I have been busy travelling throughout the world preaching the Dharma. There are always thousands of people who attend these events; however, I regret that I have no way of talking to every individual devotee and friend directly and leisurely. By dedicating this book to them, I hope that it can serve as a bridge to connect our hearts together, and thus, to some degree, reduce my regret.
3. In modern education there is a serious lack of books that encourage and promote learning and the cultivation of body and mind. I hope that this book can be used as a reference and guidebook to cultivating the mind for numerous students, and that it can profoundly influence their future.
4. *Roots of the Dharma*, like the old *The Vegetable Root Sayings*, is not like delicious gourmet food, but rather like the plain vegetables that go with the simple meal. I hope readers can be spiritually invigorated and completely relaxed and happy at this humble table.

Hsing Yun
Hsi Lai Temple
Los Angeles
August 1998

Acknowledgements

We wish to thank all those who had helped made this book possible. First and foremost, our greatest gratitude are extended to the husband and wife translating team, Dr. Tom Manzo and Dr. Shujan Cheng.

We also like to thank Venerable Miao Chieh, Susan Tidwell, and Amy Lam for their dedicated efforts during the translation process. Our appreciation also goes to everyone who has supported this project from its conception to completion.

1.

Among all forms of happiness
None is happier than harmony.
Among all enjoyments
None is more enjoyable than peace.

2.

Cultivating one day,
You gain one day's worth;
Not cultivating one day,
You gain one day's waste.
Real cultivation is in daily life;
The Buddhist way is in living life.

Hsing Yun

3.

As big as a person's heart is—
His career will be that big.
As much as a person can tolerate in his heart—
His accomplishment will be just the same.

4.

A person's accomplishment depends
On daily accumulation;
A person's success depends
On perseverance.

5.

Be one world, one act, one mind;
Do, say and write;
Observe people, self, mind.

6.

People can be poor, but not poor in mind;
The energy from the mind is boundless.
Body can be disabled, but not the mind;
Health of mind is boundless.

7.

Observing precepts is:
I am free, he is free,
Everybody is free.
I am safe, he is safe,
Everybody is safe.
I am happy, he is happy,
Everybody is happy.
I am wholesome, he is wholesome,
Everybody is wholesome.
I am benefited, he is benefited,
Everybody is benefited.
I am liberated, he is liberated,
Everybody is liberated.

8.

Cultivate body and mind to improve yourself—
Use the spirit of courtesy to deal with people—
Use high virtue to serve society—
Use farsight to observe the world—
Then you can live a fulfilled life.

9.

When people are in fortunate circumstances,
They often have their heads turned by success.
Knowing one's duty
Is the foundation of dealing with people.
When people are in adverse circumstances,
They usually are discouraged and lose ambition.
Making earnest effort to cultivate virtue
Is the foundation for handling affairs.

10.

Being
—Content in heart and accepting,
Let the fickleness of human nature be;
—Optimistic, energetic and carefree,
Don't be afraid of outside forces and political power;
—Dignified in every daily activity,
Don't live an extravagant life;
—Practicing the noble eight-fold path,
Let compassion, joy and giving run unbounded.

11.

By learning cultivation
You will develop a better temperament.
By increasing tolerance
You will nurture greater affinity with others.

12.

In the human world, there is no one inferior
To self.
In the universe, there is no where that cannot be
The pure land.

13.

The Humanistic Buddha will not abandon
Even one
Of the myriad living beings—
Because everyone has the Buddha nature.
Humanistic Buddhism will not discard
Even one
of the teachings of the world—
Because everywhere holds truth.

14.

When you are not as good as others
Don't feel self-pity;
You should know that there is a sky
Beyond the sky that you can see.
When you are better than others
Don't feel self-pride;
You should remember that there are people
Beyond the people that you can see.

15.

Don't be afraid of not having a bosom friend;
Do be afraid of the path that is not achieved.
Don't be afraid of not having a future,
Do be afraid of determination that is not strong.

16.

Don't worry,
Don't be afraid—
Making earnest effort to cultivate
And resolving deeply to succeed
Is the best medicine for eliminating illness.
Don't reject,
Don't resist—
Letting go of attachments
Is the number one secret
For eliminating irritation.

17.

You have strength, but
Don't use it to highlight others' weaknesses.
You are ignorant, but
Don't use it to ignore others' abilities.

18.

Entering the secular life, possessing
Is happiness.
But possession
Is a burden, a liability.
Leaving the secular life, emptiness
Is happiness.
Emptiness is boundless, limitless.

19.

Having roots in your heart,
You can blossom and bear fruit.
Having hope in your heart,
You can achieve professional success.
Having reason in your heart,
You can travel all over the world.
Having focus in your heart,
You can stand true.
Having virtue in your heart,
You can tolerate all things.
Having the path in your heart,
You can embrace everything.

20.

Using power to defeat people
Is momentary—
The effect is shallow.
Using virtue to influence people
Is enduring—
The effect is profound.
Better to influence people through virtue
Than to use power to defeat them.
Better to use virtue to handle affairs
Than to use power to control them.

21.

Use others' experience as
A reference for self.
Use others' success as
A model for self.

22.

Don't slander others' good reputation
To achieve your own good.
Don't discard world justice
To conceal your own error.

Hsing Yun

23.

In your heart,
Be grateful often
For the special kindness of others.
In your mouth,
Praise often
The strength of others.

24.

Replacing jealousy with praise
Makes everything joyful and complete.
Replacing attachment with acceptance
Makes everywhere convenient and at ease.

Hsing Yun

25.

Only through determination can the world
See beyond near or far.
Only through willingness can human life
See beyond suffering or happiness.

26.

Cultivating oneself
With modesty and tolerance,
One will enjoy the limitless chiliocosms
In a state
Of non-demanding and non-gaining.
Harmonizing with people
Through sacrifice and dedication,
One will attain limitless and boundless inner bliss
In a state
Of non-conflict.

Hsing Yun

27.

Only through determination
Can the failure in the past
Be the mirror of the behavior in the future.
Only through perseverance
Can the moment of obstacle
Be the power to promote success.

28.

Failure is not shameful;
Having no determination is.
Success is not joyful;
Only safety is to be congratulated.

29.

Taking initiative is like boiling water;
One must add fuel continuously
For the water to boil—
Practicing is like walking;
One must watch each step
For the action to be correct—
Taking initiative and practicing
Are the main ingredients for a successful career.

30.

Bearing difficult duties
One must have strength
But not temper;
Dealing with difficult people
One must have understanding
But not words;
Practicing a difficult path
One must have faith
But not fear;
Enduring difficult suffering
One must have tolerance
But not complaint.

Hsing Yun

31.

Disappointment—
Manage it with tolerance;
Joy—
Handle it with mildness;
Honor and favor—
Situate them with concession;
Hatred—
Settle it with retreat.

32.

With determination, one will have a goal.
With practice, one will have success.

Hsing Yun

33.

Through more tests,
One will gain more insight.
With more enjoyment,
One will lose more ambition.

34.

Those who have many desires
Are often discontent;
Discontentment leads to calamity.
Those who are content
Are usually happy;
Happiness leads to good fortune.

35.

In fortunate circumstances,
One should caution self.
In adverse circumstances,
One should strive upward.

36.

In tolerance, one should have the spirit
Of accepting difference.
In dealing with people, one should have the virtue
Of being modest and understanding.
In a career, one should have the willingness
Of "who else but me?" initiative.

37.

Be
  —compassionate people through equality;
  —earth people through coexistence;
  —wise people through understanding;
  —patient people through strength;
  —affinity-forming people through giving;
  —cultivated people through purity;
  —happy people through joy;
  —Fo Guang people through harmony.

Humble Table, Wise Fare

38.

Safety is nothing more
Than contentment.
Danger is nothing more
Than gossiping.
Merit is nothing more
Than giving.
Happiness is nothing more
Than inner bliss through meditation.

39.

Having determination has nothing to do
With age.
Having reasoning has nothing to do
With loudness.
Having willingness has nothing to do
With verbal expression.
Having talent has nothing to do
With current activity.

40.

Helping others' good wishes—
The virtue is boundless.
Helping others to complete good deeds—
The contribution is multiplied.

41.

Greatness is accumulated by blood and sweat;
The more sacrifice the greater it is.
Success is attained by diligence;
The more hard work, the more successful it is.

42.

Life with suffering and happiness
Is full;
Life with success and failure
Is reasonable;
Life with gain and loss
Is fair;
Life with birth and death
Is natural.

Hsing Yun

43.

Busyness, like the sharp sword of wisdom,
Can cut the vines of false thought.
Busyness, like the Midas touch,
Can transform decay into wonder.
Busyness, like a nutritive tonic,
Can invigorate life.

44.

Having Ch'an, just like
Having flowers,
Can make fragrance more fragrant.
Having Ch'an, just like
Having landscape,
Can beautify the surroundings.
Having Ch'an, just like
Having oil and salt,
Can enhance flavor.
Having Ch'an, just like
Having sunshine,
Can shine on the past and mirror the present.

45.

Being old is not about age;
What is to be most feared is
Mind-strength decaying.
Being small is not about size;
What is to be most feared is
Principle that is not firm.

46.

You can see one's ability to handle affairs
Through one's conduct.
You can observe one's virtue and cultivation
Through one's manner of conversing.

Hsing Yun

47.

Being humble in front of people—
The passage will be open wherever you go.
Being arrogant in front of people—
It is difficult to move even one step.

48.

Buddha liberates a myriad of beings
In this Saha world;
Avalokiteshvara appears and preaches
In every concern;
Ksitigarbha goes to the hell realms
To help and save beings;
Vimalakirti goes to the human world
To promote Dharma and convert people.

49.

Buddha is in the heart;
The path is now.
Ch'an is the cessation of thoughts;
Compassion is within wisdom.

50.

Mud can grow a lotus flower;
A humble family can cultivate a worthy son;
A furnace can forge iron and steel;
Hardship can shape a great man;
Bitterness can conceal sweetness;
Worry can transform into Bodhi.

Hsing Yun

51.

The dust on the mirror will be gone
Once you wipe and polish.
The darkness in the big earth will be illuminated
Once the sun comes out.
A palm tree with no center will be nothing
Once you peel it apart.
The torch in the wood will be extinguished
Once it is withdrawn.
All flowers blossoming in spring will fade
Once the wind blows.
The ice in extreme winter will melt
Once spring comes.
The false thought of beings will disappear
Once one is enlightened.
The obsessed and muddled mind will understand
Once people have demonstrated.

52.

Calmness is the door to wisdom;
Diligence is the seed to success;
Gratefulness is the fountain of happiness;
Repentance is the prescription for error.

53.

Have faith in the Triple Gem;
Have the path in your heart;
Have compassion for all beings;
Have enthusiasm for Buddhism;
Have, especially, the spirit of undying dedication
To Buddhism.

54.

Don't just look at yourself,
Look at others.
Don't just look at now,
Look at the future.
Don't just do one thing,
Do many things.
Don't just listen to one word,
Listen to many words.

55.

Implementing as soon as knowing
Is brilliant;
Implementing without knowing
Is mediocre;
Knowing without implementing
Is stupid;
Neither knowing nor implementing
Is to not accomplish anything.

56.

Hope can set your mind to tomorrow;
Action must be carried out today.

57.

Be like pines and cedars—
They can endure trials;
Be like organs and their senses—
Each has its own duty;
Be like the blind and the lame—
They can help each other;
Be like sages and the wise—
They do not look down upon beginners.

58.

Don't be afraid of criticism;
Be afraid of flattery.
Don't be afraid of failure;
Be afraid of ignorance.

59.

Reforming one's mind and personality
Is the medicine for changing destiny;
Repenting and transforming one's self
Is the prescription for creating destiny.

60.

Everyone is the artist for their own life,
And can paint their own life-world;
Everyone is the engineer for their own life,
And can build their own nice image.

61.

Being tolerant, every road is wide;
Being critical, everywhere is thorny.

62.

Immoral knowledge and view seem right
But are wrong;
They make people sink into perversion.
Right knowledge and view
Clear the mind;
They make people at ease.

63.

Honesty is the Dharma place;
Frankness is pure land;
Happiness is wealth;
Modesty is the crown.

64.

Language
—Should be like sunshine
And produce a bright view.
—Should be like a flower
And produce fragrant thought.
—Should be like clean water
And produce clear ideas.

Hsing Yun

65.

Enjoying health is not as good as
Enjoying safety.
Enjoying wealth is not as good as
Enjoying the fragrance of books.
Enjoying fame and fortune is not as good as
Enjoying without demands.
Enjoying possessing is not as good as
Enjoying non-demanding.

66.

Willing to learn and do is capable.
Neither willing to learn nor to do is ignorant.

67.

Being honest and considerate is not easy to fake;
The test is time.
Being treacherous and preposterous is not inborn;
The test is gains and losses.

68.

Reciting the Buddha's name should be
Natural and happy;
Practicing meditation should be
Free of mind and liberating;
Living life should be
Complete and at ease;
Teaching Dharma should be
Observant of the whole world and universe.

69.

Dharma has no evil or right;
If the mind is evil, then every Dharma is evil;
If the mind is upright, then every Dharma is right.

70.

Improper wealth is a poisonous snake.
Proper, clean wealth is a resource.

71.

Belief is
—Like starlight, it brightens the road;
—Like a mansion, stable and safe;
—Like a big ship, traversing the ocean;
—Like the company of good friends.

72.

The brave create destiny;
The weak rely on destiny;
The kind observe destiny;
The wise change destiny.

73.

Being honest with people is a virtue;
It gains people's respect.
Being critical is a vice;
It gains people's dislike.

74.

Dealing with people and handling affairs
Should be like water—
Encountering mountains, water turns;
Encountering the coast, water turns;
Encountering rocks, water turns;
No matter whom I encounter, I turn.

Hsing Yun

75.

Doing evil candidly and with no fear
Is called a big evil;
Doing good timidly
Is called a small good.

76.

Treasuring good opportunity
You will gain even more good opportunity;
Treasuring causes and conditions
You will encounter even more good causes and conditions.

Hsing Yun

77.

Looking at others' mistakes
Is the basis for incurring hostility;
Looking at one's own mistakes
Is the foundation for innumerable good.

78.

Being able to see through things
Everything is mine;
Being unable to see through things
Everything is not mine.

Hsing Yun

79.

Life with suffering and hardship
Is like a whetstone;
With more suffering, you gain more endurance;
With more hardship, you gain more perseverance.

80.

It is a pity to waste time;
It is a pity to live without learning;
It is even more of a pity to learn without accomplishing.

Hsing Yun

81.

A thought of anger—80,000 doors to obstacles open;
The sound of "Namo Buddha"
—everyone achieves Buddhahood.
We should be careful with every thought;
Place yourself within compassion and wisdom.

82.

If you forgive yourself all the time
You will always lose yourself;
If you are kind to yourself everywhere
You will often lose yourself.

83.

Be a morally upright person;
Dare to speak, dare to act.
Don't be a passive person,
Careless and mediocre.

84.

In human life motivate others;
Don't be the one that others pity.

Hsing Yun

85.

To be successful
One must strive.
To be able to strive
One must have a sense of shame.

86.

Look at the bright side;
Think about the big picture;
Observe the details;
Explain the profound.

87.

Wasting away the time
Is ruining yourself;
Wasting energy
Is trampling upon yourself.

88.

Illness is the shortcut for approaching
The essence of the path.
Suffering is the opportunity to approach
Deep resolve.
Busyness is the artery to approach
Values.
Lacking is the stepping stone for approaching
Completion.

89.

The viewpoint from sincerity
Is great viewpoint;
The responsibility in affliction
Is great responsibility.

90.

Being able to know humiliation
One can become a great talent.
Being able to know self weaknesses
One can become a perfect person.

91.

Cultivate one's actions;
Cultivate one's speech;
Cultivate one's Buddha mind;
Cultivate self;
Cultivate healthy relations with others;
Cultivate whenever and wherever one may be;
Cultivate without claiming merit;
Cultivate good fortune;
Cultivate wisdom;
Cultivate through Ch'an and the Pure Land teachings.

92.

In handling affairs you should have the spirit
Of battling.
In cultivating you should have the determination
To subdue demons.

93.

Good medicine is hard to take
But is good for illness;
Living a simple life
And showing one's true goal
Is good for one's career.
Honest advice is hard to take
But is good for conduct;
Being pure and non-demanding
Is good for the mind.

94.

The dragon must swim
To the big ocean
To contend with crashing waves
So that it can move at ease.
The lion must run
To the jungle
To defeat all animals
So that it can show its valiant look.
The bird must fly
To the limitless sky
To accept challenge
So that it can learn to wheel about at pleasure.
The human must enter
The society
To endure tests
So that he can grow rapidly.

95.

Supernatural power cannot hold up against Karma.
Supernatural power cannot compare with Virtue.
Supernatural power cannot compete with Emptiness.

96.

Sudden causes and conditions—
Hold on to every bit of them;
One moment of immediate presence
Transcends thousands of years.
One moment is no different from thousands of years.
A room dark for thousands of years—
Illuminate it with only one light;
Passing through thousands of years
Everything is at just one moment.
Thousand of years are no different from one moment.

Hsing Yun

97.

Firm belief exists in the sincerity of one thought;
With the deep sincerity of one thought
Everything can be touched.

98.

Every moment is a dawn,
Every challenge an opportunity,
Every adverse circumstance a test,
Every good deed a creation.

Hsing Yun

99.

Only by cherishing strength,
Conserving and storing it up,
Can one amass the force ready to strive
To realize the ideal.
Only by cherishing all affinities
Respectfully and tolerantly,
Can one work as a team with others
To accomplish good things together.

100.

Sacrificing one's life for a just cause—
Although one dies,
The spirit will be eternal.
Struggling indiscriminately to survive—
Although one lives,
The spirit is gone.

Hsing Yun

101.

From the appearances of Buddha and the Sangha,
See the original demeanor of self.
From the flowers, grass, sand and rocks,
Familiarize yourself with chiliocosms.
From the prayer mat and prostration cushion
Examine the limitless life of self.
From the calm night and bright moon,
Have firm confidence in the eternal future.

102.

The unrefined compete with others
Over strength.
The ignorant compete with others
Over anger.
The wise compete with others
Over wisdom.
The sagacious compete with others
Over determination.

Hsing Yun

103.

In fortunate circumstances
Don't have your head turned by success;
In adverse circumstances,
Don't have indiscreet conduct.
In other words,
Don't lose determination when poor,
Don't be defiant when rich.

104.

Being tolerated
Reveals how small self is;
Forgiving others
One can enlarge self.

Hsing Yun

105.

Poverty is the gem stone
to polish determination;
Wrongful accusation is the winter snow
To mature body and mind;
Adverse circumstances are the exam papers
To test life;
Worry is the resource
To cultivate the right path.

106.

The best gift is good advice;
The best cultivation is forgiveness.

107.

The wise repent and mend their ways;
The ignorant conceal their errors with excuses.
By mending your ways, your virtues
Will be improved daily.
By concealing your errors, your vices
Will accumulate daily.

Humble Table, Wise Fare

108.

Earnestly mending one's way
One will achieve great goodness;
Taking in the future
One will have great determination.

Hsing Yun

109.

One should:
Make a great pledge;
Form moderate affinity;
Expect little blessing.
One should:
Choose a high point to stand on;
Find level ground to sit on;
Aim for broad places to proceed.

110.

Making a fortune is not as good as
Taking initiative;
Changing your destiny is not as good as
Reforming your mind;
Taking charge of the world is not as good as
Taking charge of the mind;
Saving people is not as good as
Saving minds.

Hsing Yun

111.

Being blamed and scolded—
Without resentment,
One can increase wisdom and merits.
Being praised—
And feeling proud of it,
Will conceal some crisis.

112.

For people who are good at studying,
Everything is under their control;
For people who like to pay respect to Buddha,
Any worry cannot gain entry.

Hsing Yun

113.

Believing in religion blindly is not worrisome
Because people just do not understand;
Not believing in religion is sorrowful
Because people have nothing to gain;
Believing in religion wrongly is fearful
Because people will fall into the wrong path;
Believing in religion correctly is joyful
Because people will have a bright future.

114.

The more difficulty and frustration one experiences
The more one will have
An inverse increase in greater opportunities.
Learning everything
With mindfulness and earnest diligence
One will be able to break through limits.

Hsing Yun

115.

By not being affected
By others' slandering your good name
You can say you thoroughly understand life;
By not making joy and anger
Visible
You can say you are perfectly cultivated.

116.

Dharma is not pursuing mystery;
Only with the right path
Can it liberate self and others;
The path is not pursuing quick achievement;
Only with determination
Can it be profound and lasting.

Hsing Yun

117.

The best method to solve difficulties
Is to overcome them through great endeavor;
The best method to obtain happiness
Is to give it to people wholeheartedly.

118.

One would rather be lonesome
For a moment
Than be miserable for a lifetime;
One would rather keep the path
For a lifetime
Than be unclear for a moment.

Hsing Yun

119.

    Sand can cultivate seedlings of grain;
    Mud can grow a pure lotus;
    Whether outside circumstances are good or bad
    Is unimportant;
    What is important are useful seeds.

Humble Table, Wise Fare

120.

Feel grateful to others often;
Only fear not doing enough good.
Think humbly of self often;
Only fear not eliminating vices timely enough.

Hsing Yun

121.

Be joyful, but don't laugh out loud;
Be angry, but don't fly into a rage;
Be sad, but don't wail a lot;
Be happy, but don't be frivolous.

Humble Table, Wise Fare

122.

Doing your best—though you fail
You still succeed;
Winning through sheer luck—though you succeed
You actually fail.

Hsing Yun

123.

Making spiritual progress
Is the only method for developing hidden talent;
Repentance is the concrete action
For cutting off vices and seeking after the good.

124.

Pursuing knowledge should have insight;
Relationships with others should show common sense;
Character should have experience and understanding;
Seeking the path should be proper and right.

Hsing Yun

125.

One should prefer to create
The opportunities for causes and conditions
Rather than sit and wait
For causes and conditions to work.

126.

Hearing more is not as good
As seeing more;
Talking more is not as good as
Doing more;
Doubting more is not as good as
Inquiring more;
Worrying more is not as good as
Taking more precautions.

Hsing Yun

127.

The purpose of speaking is not to display self
But to inspire others;
The purpose of doing is not for personal gain,
With little thought for others,
But to serve everyone.

128.

One who is generous will be able
To gather people;
One who is disciplined will be able
To earn people's respect;
One who is tolerant will be able
To win people over;
One who is advancing will be able
to lead people.

Hsing Yun

129.

By harmonizing your mind and doing good
You will feel at ease;
Then, naturally, your body will be healthy.
By forming good affinities widely
You will have more opportunities;
Then, naturally, your wealth will be broad.

130.

Learning to "pick it up" and "let it go"
Can enlarge the breadth of your mind;
Being able to see far and do the right thing
Can improve your life.

Hsing Yun

131.

Being serene is more important than
Social climbing;
Making concessions is more important than fighting;
Having relationships based on the same beliefs
Is more important than
Human warmth;
Pleasure from Dharma is more important than
Pleasure from desire.

132.

Following opportunity naturally
Is not following trends blindly—
It is cherishing the very moment.
The very moment is not in a pureland—
It is simply a thought at heart.

Hsing Yun

133.

Following opportunity naturally
Everything will be settled;
Try to minimize daily expenses.
Doing everything based on the precepts
You will have no worry naturally.

134.

Excellent acting comes from actors
Who seriously understand the content of the role;
Plentiful life must come from one
Who strives to personally verify the meaning of life.

Hsing Yun

135.

Understanding how the Dharma applies
To daily life
One will have the means to follow
Opportunity and one's life at ease;
Looking at everything
Through the Dharma viewpoint
One will have the means to deal
With changeable life.

136.

Worshipping a deity is a moment of respect;
Taking refuge is a lifetime belief.

Hsing Yun

137.

    Making prostrations can defeat one's self-pride;
Chanting the Buddha's name
Can subdue false thought;
Doing good can stop greed and desire;
Being tolerant
Can cure anger and hatred.

138.

Courtesy is the safeguard for peace;
Without courtesy, there will be crises.
Precepts are the support for safety and happiness;
Without precepts, there will be chaos.

139.

Repentance is not just bodily prostration;
It is examining one's mind critically.
Repentance is not just a moment of confession;
It is a lifetime of removing filth.

140.

Repentance can make people's minds
fresh and cool;
Taking initiative can make people's determination
Strong and firm.

Hsing Yun

141.

Repentance, like clear water,
Can clean the three karmas
And the obstacles of doing evil.
Repentance, like clothing,
Can make our body, mind and virtue
August.

142.

The decayed scab should be removed
So that the new flesh can grow;
Bad habits should also be removed
So that one can cultivate virtue.

Hsing Yun

143.

Arrogant manner—should not grow;
Integrity—cannot do without;
Greedy thoughts—should not have;
The mind seeking enlightenment—cannot be lacking.

144.

I would rather be a flower,
Spreading fragrant air
And giving people fragrance;
I would rather be a bridge,
Linking everyone's transit
And giving people convenience;
I would rather be a tree,
Protecting thousands of pedestrians
And giving cool freshness;
I would rather be a pond,
Nourishing travelers' minds
And quenching people's thirst;
I would rather be a lamp,
Illuminating the road in the darkness
And giving people brightness.

145.

Writing should have self
So that one can have viewpoint and life;
Cultivating should have no self
So that one can be awakened and enlightened.

146.

Awakening is
From the change of idea
To the transformation of taste in life;
Attainment is
From the realization of cultivation
To harmonization of the union of mind and Buddha.

Hsing Yun

147.

A grounding in Dharma is more important
Than a human grounding;
Everybody is more important
Than self;
Culture and education are more important
Than charity;
Having the path is more important
Than having wealth.

148.

When others are discouraged,
One word of encouragement can save them
At the last moment from a hopeless situation;
When others are disappointed,
One word of praise can help them
turn over a new future.

Hsing Yun

149.

With people, do good and say nice things;
Be a good person and follow naturally what is right;
With perfect willingness, do good deeds;
Have good intentions, and everyone is happy.

150.

Ears often hear good advice that is unpleasant;
Without showing anger on the face—
This is the foundation for cultivating body
And increasing virtue.
Mind often contains things that are against your will;
Without showing any unpleasant reaction in your body—
This is the root for cultivating patience
And reforming personality.

Hsing Yun

151.

Having determination and making effort—
Although one may not succeed completely,
One will make some progress.
Taking initiative and striving upward—
Although one may not realize completely,
One will make some advances.

152.

When noisy, temper your mind;
When quiet, cultivate your mind;
When sitting, guard your mind;
When walking, examine your mind;
When talking, inspect your mind;
When moving, control your mind.

Hsing Yun

153.

In studying truth, have determination;
In handling affairs, base your actions on principle;
In behavior, obey ethics;
In dealing with people, be understanding.

154.

The common consider their own faults
To be the fault of others;
They often blame everyone but themselves.
The virtuous consider others' faults
To be their own fault;
They often examine their conscience
And blame themselves.

Hsing Yun

155.

To stand out among equals
You must have firm and strong stamina;
To succeed in a career
You must have unceasing spirit.

156.

The force of a conflagration
Is kindled by a spark;
The water that destroys mountains
Is begun with a little drop of water.

Hsing Yun

157.

Faith, like a necklace of precious stones,
Makes our body and mind august.
Faith, like a walking stick,
Makes us proceed without anxiety.

158.

Pursue the path
Without care
And worry will be not be far behind.
Conduct yourself
Often at ease
And determination will not be large.

Hsing Yun

159.

Receiving through pity
Is not as good as
Being rewarded through hard work.
Being rewarded through hard work
Is not as good as
Self-obtained success.

Humble Table, Wise Fare

160.

One who can strive
Under difficult circumstances
Must have some accomplishment;
One who can create
Under ordinary circumstances
Must make some progress.

Hsing Yun

161.

To understand true self nature
One must undergo cultivation;
To understand life's original demeanor
One must go through personal verification.

162.

A thought of doing evil
May lead to a grave mistake;
A thought of repentance
May bring back life and good health.

Hsing Yun

163.

    Being deserted is the unexpected stick
    That hits and breaks
    The mentality of dependence;
    Being commended is the breeding ground
    That nurses and strengthens
    A helpless spirit.

164.

Digging a well when thirsty
Shows lack of forethought.
Being conceited and rude
Leads to few helpful opportunities.
Observing without moving forward
Increases shame and embarrassment.
Having no sense of shame or embarrassment
Brings misfortune upon the house.

Hsing Yun

165.

By retreating with caution
One can jump farther;
With proper rest
One can walk longer.

Humble Table, Wise Fare

166.

Owning the world is not wealth;
Having real spiritual substance is precious.

Hsing Yun

167.

Not accomplishing the path, the fault
Is too much indulgence and idleness.
Not accomplishing studies, the blame
Is lack of aspiration.

168.

It's okay to engage
In a humble profession.
It's okay to reside
On a little-known, narrow plot of land;
Only through contributing one's dreams
Can one live righteously and courageously.

Hsing Yun

169.

Ask for cultivating
—Without expecting harvest;
Salute others' work
—Without seeking self-happiness;
Think about giving
—Without demanding retribution;
Aspire to accomplishment
—Without calculating hard work.

170.

Don't be afraid of failure;
Only be afraid of idleness.
The more failure,
The richer the experience.

Hsing Yun

171.

Use honest advice as good medicine
To aid self and others;
Use good words as acupuncture
To benefit self and others.

172.

Words with sincerity and credibility
Will move people deeply.
Words without sincerity and credibility
Will move people—not deeply.

Hsing Yun

173.

For the poor,
Not demanding is the virtue;
For the rich,
Being able to give is the virtue;
For the highly placed,
Being courteous to others is the virtue;
For the lowly placed,
Overlooking power is the virtue.

174.

The levels of possession are limited;
The pleasure of enjoyment is limitless.

Hsing Yun

175.

The world's wealth—
Obtain with the hand of faith;
The broad river and sea—
Cross with the boat of faith;
The omniscient Buddha fruit—
Grow with the fruit of faith;
The boundless Dharma treasure—
Enter through the door of faith.

176.

Real rest
Is to rest the six organs
And stop false thoughts.
Real pleasure
Is to use Dharma to amuse oneself
And to involve education in entertainment.

Hsing Yun

177.

Always repenting
One can turn over a new life;
Always taking initiative
One can strive upward.
Repentance can remove karma
Resulting from previous sins;
Taking initiative can
Result in a future career.

178.

Contentment is a natural wealth.
Extravagance is a man-made poverty.
Making spiritual progress is a limitless resource.
Idleness is an invisible crisis.

Hsing Yun

179.

Be diligent,
And time will bring you hope;
Be idle,
And society will forget your existence.

180.

Memory is the beautiful scene at dusk.
Illusion is darkness without light.
Rational thought is the sun at high noon
Application is traveling the world.

Hsing Yun

181.

With determination
Small projects can be enlarged;
With strength,
Slander can be turned into praise.

182.

Action without results
Is the same as
Cultivation without harvest.
Language without response
Is the same as
A deserted valley without echo.

Hsing Yun

183.

The ancient Chinese regarded
Concealing the faults of others
And praising their good points
As beautiful virtue.
Buddhist disciples regard
Speaking positive words frequently
As cultivating virtue.

184.

Without courage
One cannot overcome hardships;
Without perseverance
One cannot achieve results.

Hsing Yun

185.

Holding a belief that "it is hard to come by"
One can meekly accept humiliation
And gladly consider the bitter as if it were molasses.
Endowed with the spirit of "doing good with others"
One can broadly form good affinities
And achieve the satisfaction of everyone concerned.

186.

Shouldn't say it but says it—
Saying it is reckless;
Should say it but doesn't say it—
Is concealing a villainy;
Shouldn't say it but says it—
Is making mistakes in handling affairs;
Should say it but doesn't say it—
Will make mistakes in handling people.

Hsing Yun

187.

When viciously scolded—
Be silent without seeking revenge.
When facing a setback—
Be peaceful in mind.
When hated and envied—
Treat it with compassion.
When slandered—
Remember their virtues in gratitude.

188.

In leisure—do not neglect;
It will have benefit when busy.
In secret—do not conceal;
It will have benefit when obvious.
In inactivity—do not end up in nothing;
It will have benefit when active.
In confusion—do not attach;
It will have benefit when awakening.

Hsing Yun

189.

Being involved, one can penetrate deeply;
Working hard, one can be outstanding;
Being ordinary, one can be distinguished;
Disciplining oneself, one can be skilled.

190.

Paying attention, one can discover problems.
Studying, one can resolve problems.

Hsing Yun

191.

The account book of Fo Guang Shan
Hangs on the wall;
The personnel of Fo Guang Shan
Spread all over the world.

192.

All accomplishment is obtained
Through diligence.
All failure is attained
Through idleness.

Hsing Yun

193.

Using initiative as energy
One can move forward against the current;
Using grief and indignation as strength
One can redress the wrong and restore justice.

Humble Table, Wise Fare

194.

One would rather keep the path
And die of poverty and humility—
Than live with wealth and honor
Without it.
One would rather die
From upholding the precepts
To improve virtue—
Than live successfully
Without them.
Having the path or not,
Having the teachings or not,
Is the distinction between
The virtuous and the common.

Hsing Yun

195.

Experience comes from personal application.
Success results from vigorously striving.
One cannot cultivate honesty
Without thrift;
One cannot make up for lack of talent
Without diligence.

Humble Table, Wise Fare

196.

The orchid is hidden in the secluded valley;
Pearls are hidden in the ocean depths;
Precious jade is hidden in painstaking polishing;
Steel is hidden in hammering and shaping;
Great minds are hidden in slow maturity;
Success is hidden in modesty and humiliation;
The sage and the virtuous are hidden in narrow plots;
The wisest are hidden in the most foolish.

Hsing Yun

197.

Saying nice words—
Compassionate, loving words
Are like winter sun;
Encouragement and praise
Are just like flowers that
Are fragrant everywhere;
Doing good deeds—
Is as easy as raising a hand,
But the virtue is wonderful;
Dedication and service
Are just like a full moon that
Illuminates in the high sky;
Having good intentions—
Sincerity and good affinities
Are good fortune;
With the sage and the virtuous in mind,
Is just like a good harvest from a good farm.

198.

The body is the phenomenon
Of four elements;
Besides the physical body
There is an undying life
That is our spiritual body.
Wealth and properties are possessed
By five classes jointly;
Besides outside wealth
There is an eternal treasure
That is our true feelings.

About the Author

Venerable Master Hsing Yun was born in Chiangsu Province, China in 1927 and entered a monastery near Nanjing at age twelve. He was fully ordained in 1941, and is the 48th patriarch of the Lin-chi (Rinzai) Ch'an school. In 1949, amid the turbulence of civil war, he went to Taiwan.

Venerable Master Hsing Yun is the founder of the Fo Guang Shan (Buddha's Light Mountain) International Buddhist Order, which is headquartered in Taiwan and supports temples worldwide. The order was founded in 1967 and emphasizes education and public service.

For nearly half a century, Venerable Master Hsing Yun has devoted his efforts to transforming this world through the practice of Humanistic Buddhism. He reminds us that to transform our world, we must be actively engaged in it. We can realize our true nature in the here and now, within this precious human birth and this world. When we actualize altruism, joyfulness, and universality, we are practicing the fundamental concepts of Humanistic Buddhism.

Dr. Tom Manzo's credentials include a Ph.D. from Yale University, in Literature. He received his Bodhisattva Precepts in 1997 on his first visit to Hsi Lai Temple. Currently, he is a faculty member at San Antonio College, Texas. Dr. Shujan Cheng, married to Dr. Tom Manzo, holds a Ph.D. degree in Finance. Originally from Taiwan, she has been a resident in the U.S. for the past ten years. A Buddhist for many years, she received her Bodhisattva Precepts several years ago.

Glossary

Avalokiteshvara: The Bodhisattva of Great Compassion; also known as the Kuan Yin, the goddess of mercy. A Bodhisattva is a being who has almost become a Buddha, but who has chosen to remain in the Saha world in order to help other sentient beings.

Chiliocosms: Buddhism believes that there are an almost infinite number of worlds, with an almost infinite number of sentient beings; each sentient being possesses the Buddha nature and therefore can achieve enlightenment, though perhaps not in their present existence.

Five classes: The five classes are rulers, thieves, flood, fire, and prodigal sons; who have the wealth struggled for by others as their common prey.

Four elements: The four elements are earth, water, fire, and air.

Hell realms: Buddhism, being rational accepts that a being's karma (thoughts, words and deeds) will cause appropriate effects to be (sooner or later) visited upon the being. At death, any left-over karma of the previous life, or lives, may begin to blossom; therefore, Buddhism admits of many realms of hell and heaven.

Ksitigarbha: The Bodhisattva of Great Vows; he vowed to delay becoming a Buddha until all sentient beings in the hell realms were saved.

Namo Buddha: To take refuge in the Buddha.

Pure Land: Pure Lands are presided over by certain Buddhas where moral or spiritual conditions of development predominate.

Saha: The world where all sentient beings live.

Three karmas: The three karmas result from thought, words and deeds.

Vimilakirti: The enlightened lay Buddhist, emphasizing that the lay life is not necessarily an impediment to enlightenment.